629.22 Monroe, Lynn Lee.
M
      Boneshakers and
      other bikes

DATE		

First Pedaled Bicycle ~ ~ Boneshaker ~ ~ Ariel ~

Club Convertible ~ ~ Racing Ordinary ~ ~ Tricycle ~

pictures by George Overlie

BONESHAKERS AND OTHER BIKES

by Lynn Lee Monroe

LERNER PUBLICATIONS COMPANY ■ MINNEAPOLIS, MINNESOTA

How fast can you run? Faster than a dog? A horse? A deer? No, neither you nor I can run that fast. As soon as we've run for just a little while, we puff and pant. If we traveled just on our own two feet, we'd stay very close to home.

What if we had no cars or buses or trains or airplanes? Not too long ago people didn't. Then, if someone wanted to visit a friend or go to a special birthday party, he had to walk—no matter how far—or ride on horseback, or drive a horse-drawn carriage.

But horses were a lot of trouble, and imaginative people dreamed of something better—something that didn't eat or drink; something that wouldn't get scared or mean. Wouldn't a *mechanical* horse be better, they thought.

Inventive people did more than dream. They tried to *build* such a marvelous machine.

French Hobbyhorse - 1791

The great-granddaddy of what later became known as the "bicycle" originated in France. Because it looked like a toy horse on wheels, it was called the "hobbyhorse." People made this two-wheeler go by pushing their feet along the ground. They could not steer it, so they had to go straight forward. This meant that the hobbyhorse riders could never turn corners. Even if a dog darted out in front of them, they could not swerve away. But they *could* travel faster on the hobbyhorse than they could on foot—at least if they didn't try to climb a hill. If people wished a more unusual mount than a horse, they could ride a snake or a lion. On bonny days, dashing young Frenchmen rode their carved animals-on-wheels in the park.

Forester's Bicycle - 1817

Years later, there lived a man in Germany who was chief forester for a duke. The duke owned miles and miles of forest, and he did not want other people shooting his animals or cutting down his trees. So the forester's job was to hike up the steep hills, down the deep valleys, and along the twisting, turning paths of the forest—mile after mile every day—guarding the forest from trespassers and thieves. What a boring, exhausting job! The forester didn't want to tramp all day long. He wanted time to invent contraptions, to tinker with wood and metal, and odds and ends. The forester wanted to buy a speedy horse, but all of his money went for parts for inventions. Finally, the forester decided what to do. What he did was to invent a contraption made of two carriage wheels with a high wooden "backbone," or bar, between them. So that he could *steer* his machine, the forester attached a handlebar to the front end of the backbone and connected it to the front wheel. Riding on his wooden horse, the forester could travel along the paths of the forest in only half the time and with only half the effort of walking. Now he was no longer so weary, and he had plenty of time to tinker.

The first time the forester strode into town on his strange contraption, the children scurried away in terror. But soon they danced with glee as they watched the fat little forester "prance" by on his odd wooden horse. The old town fathers, however, scorned such nonsense. In fact, they threatened to chase the forester out of town if he clanked his rattling iron wheels on the cobblestone streets any longer.

But before long, the forester's bike became quite popular. Soon, many wealthy young men wearing stylish clothes and tall hats rode improved hobby-horses like the forester's along park walks and roadways. Since these fancily dressed young men were called "dandies," the mechanical horses they rode were called "dandy horses."

The ladies wanted to join in the fun. But they could not ride the dandy horse because their long full skirts got in the way of the high bar between the wheels. So a special dandy horse was made just for them. The ladies' dandy horse had a lowered bar with a high seat attached to it.

Ladies' Dandy Horse
1818

There were certain drawbacks to riding the dandy horse. Because dandy horses were made of heavy wood and iron, the riders had to be strong and healthy or they would puff and pant as they pushed along. But of course, not everyone was in top physical condition, so riding the dandy horse was too strenuous for some people. Shoe leather was another problem. Because the riders pushed their bikes with their feet, huge holes were worn in the soles of their shoes. And then there were muddy roads. As the riders plopped one foot after the other into the muck, their fine clothes soon looked like dirty rags.

Most people thought the riders looked ridiculous on their bikes. So they would point at the dandies and snicker at them whenever the riders strode by. As if that wasn't bad enough, newspapers drew silly cartoons that made the dandies look stupid riding their "horses." Would you like to be chased or laughed at all the time? Neither did the dandies. Soon, nobody cared to ride a dandy horse anymore.

In the days of the dandy horse, nobody dreamed a rider could balance on two wheels without his feet touching the ground. But several years later, a Scotchman attached pedals to the rear wheel of his bicycle. Now he could really speed along, and his feet never touched the ground. He didn't wear out his shoe leather, and he didn't get muddy.

The local judge called the Scotchman the devil himself, for no flesh-and-blood human being could sit on top of a wheel without falling! But the Scotchman was no devil. He was simply the first person to pedal a bicycle.

First Pedaled Bicycle 1839

The Scotchman was a showoff who delighted in shocking people with his tricks. Once, he held a little girl on his shoulder while steering his wooden horse with only one hand. Another time, he coasted down a hill very swiftly while standing on the saddle of his bike. Then, he was almost arrested by policemen for *riding* on a *foot*path. But the smart Scotchman so entertained the policemen with his fancy riding tricks that they clapped their hands for him and let him go scot-free.

In all the world, this Scotchman was the only person to own a two-wheeler with pedals. But when he stopped riding his bicycle, nobody remembered the pedals he invented. So pedals had to be invented all over again.

One day, about 20 years later, a French carriage repairman stared at an old hobbyhorse someone had brought to him for repair. This old two-wheeler had to be pushed by foot. Surely there must be an easier way, he thought. After tinkering quite a bit, the Frenchman thought of pedals to turn the front wheels. Now his two-wheeler worked much easier.

Boneshaker 1861

But his bicycle had one serious fault—the wheels were made of hard wood with iron around the rims. What a rough ride! Can you imagine bouncing bump, bump, BUMP over rough cobblestone roads? No wonder people nicknamed this contraption the "boneshaker"!

As bike riders bounced along on their boneshakers, they couldn't help but wonder how the jolting and jarring could be stopped. One day an American was wondering about it, too, as he swayed and bumped along. "Surely," he thought, "all this shaking up isn't good for my innards. I may be shaking my heart—or my liver—right out of place! How can I get a smoother ride?" Suddenly an idea popped into his head—use *rubber* wheels instead of wooden ones. And his idea worked— rubber tires gave a much, much more comfortable ride. At last, his insides could remain where they belonged.

Ariel - 1870

Yet, the wood-and-iron boneshakers, even with rubber tires, were heavy and cumbersome—especially if you had to climb a hill. So an English inventor built a lighter bicycle of metal and rubber. He named it the "Ariel," which means "as light and feathery as a fairy sprite."

The Ariel had a high front wheel that made the bicycle go faster. But the seat was so high that riders had to climb up a step to reach it. Soon, many men—not just the rich—rode the new high-wheeled bicycle. The Ariel and bicycles like it were nicknamed the "ordinary" because common, ordinary people rode it—not just the rich.

Club Convertible ~ 1886

But ladies could not ride the ordinary because their long skirts would tangle in the wheels. If a lady's boyfriend wanted to enjoy her company on a cycling expedition, he might buy a three-wheeled "sociable" built for two. Or he might buy a four-wheeled "club convertible," with two high wheels in the middle and a tiny wheel in front and back. Or maybe an "American Ladies' bicycle," where the lady rode sidesaddle on the back seat. Since pedaling such heavy machines was tiring for a lady, she could stop pedaling and rest while her boyfriend continued to pedal away.

Unfortunately for the ladies, not all men wanted relaxing rides. Adventurous riders wanted to cycle even faster, so they made the front wheel of the ordinary higher. Now the rider pedaled high off the ground on the tall front wheel. If he hit the tiniest bump in the road, or maybe a rock, he flew over the handlebars and hit the road head-first. Such headfirst dives, called "headers," were a common hazard that sent some riders to the hospital with smashed noses or cracked skulls. But despite these hazards, it must have been exciting to survey the world from such lofty heights.

Before long, daredevils started racing these speedy bikes. Tall men on the high wheels swayed crazily as they pedaled harder and harder. Yet racers wanted to go faster and faster, so the front wheel of the ordinary became higher and higher and HIGHER.

Racing Ordinary 1879

As the front wheel became enormous, nobody knew how to climb up to the seat. A person needed legs as long as a giraffe's neck to even reach the pedals! Soon, only the very tallest men raced the ordinaries.

Tricycle
1877

Medium-sized people tried riding "tricycles," or three-wheeled vehicles. Tricycles looked clumsy and heavy, but they could speed along, too. For awhile they were very popular, and this is how it happened. One day the Queen of England was taking a ride in her horse-drawn carriage. Suddenly, ahead of her on the road there appeared a young lady pedaling a shiny tricycle. The girl glanced over her shoulder, saw the royal coach approaching, and panicked. She bent low over the handlebars and turned the pedals as fast as they would go. Soon, the rider and the three revolving wheels whirled out of sight, far ahead of the coach. The queen was fascinated by this curious sight. She quickly discovered who the young lady was and invited her to the royal palace to demonstrate tricycling. Soon, all the princes and princesses and dukes and duchesses of England had gleaming new metal tricycles. Tricycling became quite the fashion.

But a lot of people with just middle-sized legs wanted the excitement of *bicycling* as well as *tricycling*. One lad, an English minister's son, was discouraged because his legs were too short to ride the ordinary. "*Build* a bike that you can ride," suggested his father. "Make it safe for everybody — the short, the fearful, the elderly." The minister's son did just that. His bike had a *small* front wheel and a large back wheel. The rider sat on a saddle between the wheels, so he could touch his feet to the ground if he tipped. The minister's son could now ride a bicycle, but he could not sell his invention to others. The timid and the old were too afraid to ride any bicycle at all.

For the Timid
1876

American Star
1880

Another bicycle, the "American Star," looked like a backwards ordinary: it had a large wheel on the back and a tiny wheel up front. The rider sat on the high back wheel. But because there was now more weight on the back of the bike than in the middle, the rider would accidentally jerk the front wheel off the ground and slide down the back wheel as if sliding off a bucking bronco. But surely, plopping on his seat in the road was better than getting a split skull or broken nose! But for some strange reason, the Star wasn't popular, either.

Meanwhile, the minister's son invented another bicycle—the first one with a chain and sprocket to turn the wheels. But people jeered at his crazy invention, and they nicknamed it the "crocodile." Can you guess why?

Crocodile - 1879

Finally, the bike with a chain and sprocket—called the "safety bike"—caught on. It was light in weight, and safe and easy to pedal. The rider did not swing and sway, or dive off the front, or slide off the back. He could almost always keep his balance. He could ride it no matter how tall or how short he was by raising or lowering the seat. Ladies bought safety bikes with the center bar lowered between the two wheels. A bold and brave young lady would wear bloomers, which made bike riding much easier.

Safety Bicycle
1885

Soon men and women of all ages and sizes pedaled
the new safety bike everywhere. The heyday of
bicycling was in full swing.

Besides riding bicycles, everyone tried inventing them, too. Many weird machines resulted. Some had only one wheel. Imagine yourself cycling along, perched high on top of a single wheel. Surely it takes courage to ride a "unicycle."

Or even worse, imagine yourself sitting in the middle of a gigantic wheel called a "monocycle." The revolving wheel continually whirls around your head. You have no steering wheel, so you must lean sideways to turn a corner. You have no brakes, so you must lean backwards to stop the wheel—and pray you don't fall off. And all the time you pedal along, the enormous revolving wheel spins around and around your head. Would that make you dizzy?

Monocycle
1869

French *Giraffe* 1890's

If you had the daring of a mountain climber, you might scale the oddest bike of all, the bike on stilts called the "Eiffel Tower Bike" or the "French Giraffe." Brave circus performers dared. Some, it is rumored, even pedaled this gangly contraption across a stretched tightrope.

The "bicycle built for two" was very popular. As the two cyclists pedaled along, they would sing in unison the bicycling song:

Daisy, Daisy,
Give me your answer true.
I'm half crazy
All for the love of you.
It won't be a stylish marriage.
I can't afford a carriage.
But you'll look sweet
Upon the seat
Of a bicycle built for two.

Soon, bicycles were built for three or four or five, or even more. One bicycle was built for *ten*! Can you imagine whizzing around a corner or shooting down a hill on this bike?

It was at this time, when bicycle inventing was most popular, that a new invention attracted people's attention—the automobile. Soon, people became so excited about the automobile that the bicycle was almost forgotten. Nobody worried about inventing better bikes, just better cars. So for 50 years, the safety bike was the *only* bike.

Then an Englishman invented a new kind of bike, a low bike with mini-wheels and stylish fenders and trim. At first, no factory would build the new bike. "Who would buy the little toy!" they scoffed. Finally, one factory started building the little bike. Children begged their mothers and fathers to buy it, and a brand new bicycle boom began.

Today, bicycling is more popular than ever, and for some very good reasons. Bicycles don't crowd your streets and bridges with long lines of cars. Bicycles don't pollute your ears with slamming doors, screeching brakes, rattling fenders, and beeping horns. Nor do bicycles pollute the air you breathe with smoke and soot and chemicals.

Bicycling builds strong muscles and fills your lungs with fresh air. Bicycles bring you quickly to your friend's house, or a Little League game, or the candy store. But most especially, riding your bike on a bright spring day brings color to your cheeks and joy to your heart!

Aren't you glad the bicycle was invented?